MW00579357

BREAK YOUR FAMILY INIQUITIES FOREVER!

ALI STABLEY

CREATION HOUSE
A STRANG COMPANY

BREAK YOUR FAMILY INIQUITIES FOREVER
by Ali Stabley
Published by Creation House
A Strang Company
600 Rinehart Road
Lake Mary, Florida 32746
www.creationhouse.com

Cover design by Terry Clifton

Library of Congress Control Number: 2007931862
International Standard Book Number:
978-1-59979-222-4

First Edition

07 08 09 10 11 — 987654321
Printed in the United States of America

A special thanks to **Pat Boone**, beloved American icon, who believed this book should be published, and helped make it possible.

To Chase, my son and eagle, who walked with me and suffered with me while I was overcoming, and who continues to make me proud. Chase, it is yet to be seen what footprint you will make upon the sands of time, but I believe you will fulfill John 14:12 and Joel 2.

To Mom, who had the courage to stand up and refuse to accept pain as a normal way of life in order to break the cycle of abuse in our family. Your intercession for your family paid off! I also owe her a debt of gratitude for sharing with me her huge repository of godly wisdom from her lifelong study of God's word. She was a great help in annotating this book. Thanks, Mom. I want to be just like you when I grow up!

To my brothers and sisters, Howard, Jeanette, Elaine, Donald Jr., Gloria and, Gail, who rose above the abuse to lead exemplary lives.

And to Garth, my beloved husband, who besides being my friend and covering has helped heal the hurts and calm the fears of a life that almost destroyed me. Thank you for not only encouraging me, but for making a way for me to be all God meant for me to be, and for having the 1 Corinthians 13:4 kind of love for me.

And I will restore to you the years that the locust hath eaten, the cankerworm, and the caterpillar, and the palmerworm, my great army which I sent among you.

—JOEL 2:25

CONTENTS

FOREWORD

EVERY SO OFTEN a book is produced that challenges the reader to go deeper and beyond the
surface, into the truth of why we live our lives the
way we do. Ali writes with revelation and convic-
tion about a subject very few will dare to explore.
She touches a biblical truth that she herself has had
personal experience with and how the astounding
nature of its effects on her own life nearly destroyed
her—that is, the cause-and-effect of generational
curses! She knows that if they are not dealt with,
they will destroy both you and your children for
many generations to come.

I am happy to endorse a book of this stature
because Ali uses biblical truth as her foundation, and
her personal experiences qualify her as a woman of
God who knows firsthand what it means to be delivered from the throes of generational curses. Ali's
ability to share her knowledge through the written
word, and her steadfast belief that you can break
your family's iniquities completely and forever has
brought deliverance to those who once were bound
and who are now gloriously set free.

If you are tired of going around the same mountain over and over again, or you feel that your life and the lives of your loved ones continue to repeat the same cycle of spiritual death—then this book is for you! It's a "must read' for you and all your loved ones because this book will help you find the answers you have been searching for. It will put you on the path of spiritual breakthrough, setting you free to be who you were called to be! Ali's book not only tells you *what* to do, but *how to do it*—something even some of the best books fail to do.

Once you have used this book to break free, never again will you repeat the same cycle of thinking and behavior that has prevented you from walking in newness of life! Now is the time to break free—and you have in your hands the tool that can make that happen! Go forward and be blessed as you discover the inner dealings of the issues that were once never talked about—those that have left others in a state of confusion and despair.

The time is *now* to break your family iniquities forever, and to press through to the life Christ always meant for you to have! God bless you as you embark on a journey of spiritual discovery that will change you and your family for generations to come. Eternity is waiting!

—Rev. Gail Kreason
Gail Kreason Ministries
www.gailkreason.com

CHAPTER 1

BREAK YOUR FAMILY INIQUITIES FOREVER

DID YOU EVER find yourself becoming an expert on something that you never wanted to be an expert about? John Walsh, now known as the co-founder of the National Center for Missing and Exploited Children, learned more about child predators than he ever wanted to know when his son was abducted and murdered. Candace Lightner became an expert on how the legal system handles intoxicated drivers when a drunk driver killed her daughter. She later went on to found Mothers Against Drunk Driving (MADD).

I, too, became an unwitting expert on topics I never dreamed I would have to deal with: epilepsy, personality disorders, and alcoholism. My son endured one, another decimated my marriage, and the last nearly destroyed me. The most painful things I have had to overcome have been those sin patterns, also called *iniquities* and *generational curses*, that ran in my family.

My father was an alcoholic, and both of my grandfathers died because of alcohol. An uncle committed suicide and another drank himself to death. Several other of my relatives were in a cult, and many other family members simply "lived until they died," never reaching their true potential.

I have been touched by the iniquities of my fathers, but I have determined that the iniquities will stop with me and be forever banished from my blood-line. You can do the same if you will have the faith, courage, and perseverance to follow through with the deliverance that God has for you in His Word.

CHAPTER 2

WHAT IS AN INIQUITY?

THE TERM *INIQUITY* is mentioned over three hundred times in the Bible. In most of these verses, the word *father* or *fathers* is also used. Though none of the several versions I searched mentioned generational curses, there is ample evidence in both the Old and New Testaments that believers who don't deal with family iniquities can fail to live happy, prosperous, and productive lives. They are forever battling sins over which they seem to never have victory.

There is a lot of difference between a curse and an iniquity. According to Encarta's dictionary, a curse is the supposed harm that comes from a malevolent appeal to a supernatural being. As Christians, we know that once the blood of Jesus is applied to our lives, curses pronounced over us have no effect on us. The curses mentioned in the Bible, however, are always preceded by disobedience to an oracle of God. To Christians, then, a curse is a consequence of disobedience (Prov. 26:2).

On the other hand, family iniquities are tendencies toward certain types of sin. They are cause and effect. Iniquities begin when a person continues in repeated sin—lying, cheating, or substance abuse, to name a few—to the point of addiction. What begins as a pleasurable thing eventually ends in a type of death or lawlessness (James 1:15).

If these sins remained un-dealt-with in our parents' lives, then the predisposition toward this type of sin is passed on to us. God's Word tells us that these tendencies to sin in these same areas are passed on to us "to the third and fourth generation" (Ex. 20:5). We inherit a propensity toward a certain type of sin from our ancestors. We are not punished for having a predisposition for sin because all of us are "shapen in iniquity" (Ps. 51:5), but it does behoove us to break the bonds of iniquities in order to remove any chance that we might fall into a sin that is well established in our bloodline.

We can either inherit an iniquity from our forefathers, or we can create an iniquity by having unconquered sin in our lives. When we indulge an existing propensity to sin, it often begins a pattern that is repeated until it becomes a part of our personality and way of life. It becomes an iniquity in us that we, in turn, model before our children. Thus, our children receive this same method of disobedience. You can also see how dangerous it is to recognize iniquities in our lives, yet not deal with them. When trials and tribulations come or when there are not sufficient boundaries in a person's life, the child's natural response is to act out the behavior of his or her parents, whether healthy and leading to life, or unhealthy and leading to death. This time of disobedience, or iniquity, is also translated as "lawlessness."

When Pilate was considering what to do about Jesus, the people prevailed against him, demanding that Jesus be put to death. Their hatred toward Jesus had fomented to the point that they were willing to allow the consequences of their actions—and the spirit of murder—to be handed down to their children:

> When Pilate saw that he could prevail nothing, but that rather a tumult was made, he took water, and washed his hands before the multitude, saying, I am innocent of the blood of this just person: see ye to it. Then answered all the people, and said, His blood be on us, and on our children.
>
> —MATTHEW 27:24–25

It is no mystery that as the Age of Christianity heads toward its culmination in Jesus' return the number and depth of iniquities that are acted out becomes more and more evident in our society. Lawlessness begets lawlessness. This culmination of evil in the end times is summed up as the "mystery of iniquity (2 Thess. 2:7). The fruit of the works of the flesh will keep producing more and worse fruit than the generations before (Gen. 15:16), until the world has become in such a state as to be intolerable by even the most steadfast and dedicated Christians (Matt. 24:21).

You might ask: "How can someone be saved and yet still have these family iniquities? Doesn't the blood of Jesus take care of all of our sin?"

Nearly the entire fifth chapter of Galatians talks about being in bondage to the works of the flesh. Paul admonishes us to walk in the Spirit, and he tells us that once we are free, we should strive to remain free: "Stand fast therefore in the liberty wherewith

Christ hath made us free, and be not entangled again with the yoke of bondage" (Gal. 5:1). The Apostle Paul wouldn't be telling us this if staying in that place of freedom came automatically with our salvation. So how do we refrain from going back into bondage? Paul goes on to say that we should "walk in the Spirit, and ye shall not fulfill the lust of the flesh" (Gal. 5:16).

This "walking in the Spirit" is indeed where many Christians don't spend enough time and effort. Many denominations teach that grace is all that is needed once a decision for Christ has been made, or it is not mentioned at all. In my lifetime, many of the tools and formerly ordinary aspects of worship have been removed from church services—song books have been expunged of the blood of Jesus, and instead, we sing what I call "sanitized" melodies that don't take into account the crucial work and power of the blood.

Still others rarely invoke the name of Jesus in the worship service when it is clear that there is power in His name. (See John 1:12 and Acts 4:7.) The fear of God has also been removed. Instead, we are taught only about God's mercy and grace, not about the consequences of our continued sin and iniquities. People are hungry for God, and this has created megachurches with huge memberships, but with few who truly walk holy, consecrated, and separate lives before God. It seems like no one wants to confront behavior in their congregations that is displeasing to God. That is why the Church is weak and sickly— they serve God with their lips but their hearts are far from Him (Matt. 15:8–9). Having a form of godliness on the outside, they continue to live in sin no differently than the unsaved (2 Tim. 3:4–6).

And finally, churches don't teach about the reality of hell as an actual place that many people go. (See Matthew 7:13.) Instead, they ignore the issue because it is too confrontational. People don't want to hear about hell because their sins will come before them and they will have to change. Consequently, they will no longer be able to use the excuse that "God knows my heart" when they are living in sin. Instead, they will have to confront their sin and accept the possibility that they are on the wrong road. Paul's advice in 1 Corinthians 9:27 is good for these individuals: "But I keep under my body, and bring it into subjection: lest that by any means, when I have preached to others, I myself should be a castaway."

In these final moments of time before Christ's return, it is crucial that the Church compares itself to a holy God and not the culture around it. We should be *affecting* our culture, not the other way around, as happened in Jesus' day. This means that the issue of iniquities must be addressed in the Church. The mystery of iniquity is called a *mystery* because it has to be understood, sorted out, and dealt with. It is still operating in the Church and needs to be overcome in order for the Church as a unified body to be the witness that will change our culture and reap the harvest that God intended us to have. (See Revelation 12:11.)

Some With Iniquities Escape Acting Out Behaviors

Did you ever notice that the nicest, most upstanding and law-abiding citizens can sometimes have the world's worst kids? The parents seem to do all the right things: Though they're active in their children's schools, take them to church, and do everything that a good parent should do, their kids are trouble-makers and rebellious, as far away from God as they can possibly get! Why is this true in so many Christian families? I've observed it over and over in the church families I've known and in my own extended family as well.

There are many factors that can create a rebellious child, but parents should never overlook the possi-bility of having unresolved iniquity in their family. One might say, "My kids abuse alcohol and drugs, but I never did any of those things so they didn't get it from me!" No, you may not have done those things, but iniquities are not set patterns. They are only *tendencies* toward a certain type of sin. Iniquities can even skip a generation!

In the stories of Jacob, Joseph, and Ephraim, we see that Jacob the supplanter stole his brother's birthright through deceit (Gen. 25:26–34, AMP). Jacob went on to marry Rachel, whose family served foreign gods. (See Genesis 31:34, AMP.) Jacob's son Joseph served the Living God, and was an honorable man who was second in power to the king. He was considered one of the most honorable and honest men in all of the kingdom of Egypt (Gen. 41:39–41). However, when Jacob conferred the blessing of the firstborn on Joseph's son, he chose to give this blessing to Joseph's second-born son, Ephraim, repeating the pattern that was created when Jacob stole his own brother's birthright blessing. Previously, Jacob had eradicated idol worship in his family (see Gen. 35:2). Yet, within a few generations his grandson Ephraim's offspring turned to false gods (Hosea 4:17) just like his grandmother Rachel's family, even though his father Joseph was faithful to the true and living God. Iniquities can and do skip generations.

It could be that your parents or grandparents had a proclivity toward a certain type of sin, and your children may have inherited this tendency, whether or not you gave in to this temptation. Just because a person has a tendency toward a certain type of sin does not mean that he or she will give in to that sin. Are there any sins that you have had to guard against in order to avoid falling into their temptation?

Unless and until you declare these iniquities broken off of you, your children, and your children's children, it is possible for this weakness to be transferred down your bloodline! But help is on the way. God wants to deliver you and your children from any weakness, either passive or active, that is in your family today.

That is why it is so important to look back into your family tree and see what kinds of sins beset your ancestors. Every person alive has some iniquities because we were all born into sin.

How Some Iniquities Were Acted Out in My Family

By all accounts, my father was an abusive, violent man. He did everything in his power to make my mother and his children feel wretched, even to the point of hurting us and, on several occasions, trying to kill us. He would routinely destroy what furniture we had, or throw all the light bulbs out into the street just to make our lives miserable. One time, he brought a can of gasoline and a revolver into our living room and told us he was going to kill us all.

My sweet, timid sister Elaine sneaked up behind him and withdrew the can of gas and hid it. He was so drunk that he couldn't figure out what happened to the can of gas.

One Christmas, he ripped our Christmas tree from its stand, threw it out in the back yard, and set it on fire. He did this at the exact moment that we drove into the driveway after a Wednesday evening church service so that we could all see the tree go up in flames. After my father was sure that his actions had gotten the desired effect, he retreated to his bedroom, where he drank more beer and talked to his friends on his CB radio.

This tree was actually the first Christmas tree we'd ever had. My sister Jeanette bought it with one of the first paychecks she had ever earned. Being the determined young woman that she was, Jeanette hauled that scorched and smoking stick of a tree back into the house, plugged it in, and low and behold its lights flickered on and remained lit!

We all knew that God had done something important for us that night; He'd allowed us to witness a miracle. Even though there were practically no needles left on the tree and the handmade paper garlands were either gone or ash-grey, the lights still worked.

I didn't know it then, but my father's iniquities of the "less than" mentality, depression, alcoholism, and many others were operating that night, and for all the rest of the years that he lived with us. Once my mother obtained the courage to face her fear of raising seven children alone, she divorced him. She struggled for a long time with the notion of divorce, but she knew that her children's lives were at stake.

I remember how good life became after he was gone, and I thank Mom to this day for having the guts to do what many women in the 1960s would not or could not do. Mom said, "I'd rather live in a tent with peace, than in a mansion with strife" (Prov. 17:1). We were still very poor, but we finally had peace.

What I didn't realize was that my father's propensities to sin in these areas were in me, and when I married a man who could not love me, I fell into the same patterns my father had modeled. For twelve years I was in bondage to alcohol, and many times I asked God to let me die. Sometimes, when I couldn't stand up without fear of falling, I'd cry out to God to kill me, then plead with Him to not let me die in that condition because I knew I would go to a place where I would be forever separated from Him.

I had married a man whom I later suspected had a personality disorder, and try as I might, I could not please him. His idea of a happy home was to have complete silence and total order. Everytime I tried harder to do things his way, I felt that I would lose a little more of who I was. No matter what I did to try to make our home a happy one, he always found a problem with it. One day I didn't recognize myself anymore. I eventually gave up trying to make things better. My son and I learned to simply stay out of his way. When I finally confronted him about his unusual behavior, he replied, "I wish you'd just sign the papers and get it over with." I gave him his wish so he could have the solitude and orderliness he valued above our relationship.

In the midst of this difficult season, I wrote this poem:

I want a home...
Where education is valued, not scorned;
Where spontaneity is encouraged, not
    squelched;
Where the squawk of laughter is welcomed
    over the din of television;
Where silliness and practical jokes produce
    joy instead of impatience;
Where dreams are cultivated into reality and
    creativity is rewarded;
Where happiness is a given; sadness an
    inconvenience;
Where God is acknowledged and revered.

I want a home...
Where I can be myself, no matter how tired
    or angry or frustrated I've become because
    of the toils and hassles of everyday life;
Where I can express my opinions without
    fear of being met with ridicule or hostility;
Where for the moment, I can be as lazy or as
    ambitious as I want to be;
Where I can find time to be by myself to con-
    template my future and those of the ones
    who depend on me;
Where I can show my frailties and openly
    seek the face of God;
Where I can *feel* at home, not just *be* at home;
Not just a house, I want a home.[2]

The iniquities that I had inherited from my father
and his father were the very things that made me
choose the kind of husband I did. They also kept me
in a place of helplessness, so that it looked impossible to ever get out and find a place of happiness.
Iniquities, even the ones you can't see, are respon-

sible for a great deal of the misery that are found in many relationships.

"God, all I've ever wanted to do was serve You, be a good wife, and make it to heaven! Why don't You *do* something?" was my cry.

In time, I learned that he was operating in some of the iniquities that were present in his family: control (which, through rebellion, is as the sin of witchcraft; see 1 Sam. 15:23), bitterness, unforgiveness, a "less than" mentality, dissensions, and envy, to name a few. When God finally released me from this marriage, I made a vow to take back what the devil stole! Over time, I learned that the key reason I stayed in such a destructive marriage was the un-dealt-with iniquity in my own life.

What the Devil Meant for Harm, God Turned Into Good

God had a different plan for me. I was able to see this only in hindsight, which we all know is 20/20. I had to endure the prison of sadness, need, despair, and hopelessness so that God could make me a vessel out of which He could pour the healing for other women who are just as hurting as I was. Although I would never have planned my life to include so many years of misery, I would gladly go back and walk through it again to get where I am today.

In those years that God was schooling me in the revelation of the breaking of iniquities, I finally found my purpose. Jesus became my best friend, and His Holy Spirit taught me the things that I needed to know to empower first myself and then others to break the chains of iniquities that keep good people in bad lifestyles and relationships.

I knew little about iniquities when I entered that marriage all those years ago. Had I only known, I could have saved myself twenty-seven years of misery, for that is how long I endured, trying to do the right thing by honoring my marriage covenant. My iniquities of learned helplessness, shame, self-defeating behavior, and the grasshopper complex[3] (term defined in chapter four), among others, kept me in a prison whose doors God had already unlocked.

Consider who you marry

Dr. Kelly Varner once said something so simple, yet so profound, that I wish someone had said it to me before I got married. It was this:

> The two most important things you'll ever do is choose whom you're going to marry and whom you're going to serve. But don't ever choose whom you're going to marry without first choosing the right One to serve.[4]

Even if you do choose the right one to serve, please never underestimate how important it is to check out the iniquity history of any potential mate. They don't just all magically disappear because they have made a decision for Christ. Also be careful whom you date, because every date is a potential mate. If this weren't true, why would you want to date them?

What many people do not consider when they choose their marriage partner is that they do indeed marry his or her entire family, as far as iniquities are concerned. It is a very good idea to look into the background of a potential mate to see what sorts of problems have plagued the family in years past. Questions like, are there any suicides, drug or alcohol problems, or abuse in the family history? are important ones to ask. Your prospective in-laws may think your questions strange, but to avoid this issue because you're afraid of hurting their feelings may set you up for a great deal of heartache later.

If you do marry someone whose family has been plagued by these issues, then please at least be aware that you will probably have to deal with them in your children, if not in your spouse. And if your potential mate's family has the same iniquities that are present in your family history, you will double the chances that your children will struggle in these areas. This knowledge should give you much more caution about whom you choose to marry, or date, for that matter.

Remember that you are not only choosing a mate for yourself and agreeing to deal with their iniquities, but you are choosing the parent of your children. This parent will supply not only part of their physical DNA, but their spiritual DNA as well. There is hope, though, if you are willing to break the bondage of iniquities on you and your children. This should always be done before you enter into the covenant of marriage.

My father was a violent, depraved alcoholic, yet of his seven children only two or three showed signs of being addicted to any substance. The other four fought the tendency, either consciously or subconsciously, but were never actively involved in this type of sin. Somehow, they were able to reject using drugs and alcohol as a solution to their problems, so they were never plagued with addiction issues. However, these iniquities did present themselves in some of their children's lives and required attention.

My point is that having a tendency toward a certain type of sin does not give you the excuse to commit that sin. It just means you need to be aware and take action against that particular type of sin before it manifests itself.

If you are rejecting the idea that iniquities exist, you must understand that having an iniquity in your bloodline does not mean that you are automatically going to be a *victim* of a certain type of sin. It only means that you have inherited certain weaknesses and that if you know what they are you can avoid the type of activity that would lead you down that path. This is the importance of walking in the Spirit after professing Christ. You have been given the power to overcome all things. Second Peter 2:20 says that we have "escaped the pollutions of the world through the knowledge of the Lord and Savior Jesus Christ," so it is important that you get into the Word daily. If, as the verse goes on to say, we are "again entangled therein, and [by this entanglement we are] overcome, the latter end is worse with them than the beginning." It is also imperative that we become intimate with God through frequent, fervent prayer. (See James 5:16.)

Blessings are inherited as well

This might be a good time to mention that the same law that applies to iniquities applies to the good traits of a person's bloodline as well. You read about my father's iniquities and how they affected me, my marriage, and my family, but something needs to be said about those good and righteous things that your forefathers have done as well.

Just as the propensities to sin are passed on, so are the good traits and blessings. My mother and her mother were godly women. Who knows how far back there were godly women in my heritage? However, I am sure of this: my mother has five godly daughters. Do you think this is a mere coincidence? I don't think so. We also have two godly brothers. Did we all struggle with the iniquities we inherited? You bet, but we all also have something within us that will never give up on believing that God is our source and our "present help in time of trouble" (Ps. 46:1).

We have the Lord and our godly mother to thank for that. For in those years that she battled just to keep her sanity within the confines of an incredibly abusive marriage, with no money and insufficient clothing and food, she found a refuge in God's Word. She committed much of the Bible to memory, and would often go to that place in Psalm 27 to find strength and encouragement:

> For in the time of trouble he shall hide me in his pavilion: in the secret of his tabernacle shall he hide me; he shall set me up upon a rock. And now shall mine head be lifted up above mine enemies round about me: therefore will I offer in his tabernacle sacrifices of joy; I will sing, yea, I will sing praises unto the LORD.
>
> —PSALM 27:5–6

My father was a very outgoing, verbal man. All of his co-workers and friends thought he was the greatest. He became a favorite at the bar because he routinely bought rounds of drinks for the whole house at the expense of our household's food budget. He loved to brag about his wife and family, and would often force my mother to go with him to the bars so he could show her off, as she was a beautiful, petite woman. Being the godly woman that she was, she would try to get out of going, and sometimes succeeded.

One night when I was about eleven years old, my mother refused to go to the bar with my father. He called her a pig and all other kinds of names that were untrue. After getting pathetically drunk, he came home with a special "gift" for her. It was a pig's head from the meat market. As he threw it onto the table he said, "This is you—how do you like it?"

Imagine what that did to her, and what it did to us! Because she refused to go with him to a bar, this is how he treated her. He always used opportunities like this to belittle and demean her. I spoke to her about this recently, and she said that he had a methodic campaign of cruelty against her. It was designed to diminish her moral virtue in the eyes of her children so that by comparison he would look better to us. Imagine a father using that kind of logic on his children! Imagine the damage of his words and actions, on top of the public displays of lewdness and his selfish withholding of food and clothing.

Even at his worst, though, she made a point every day to find a place alone with God, pouring out her heart so that God would give her the courage not to lash out at her abusive husband. In order to have a place of solitude, she often had to leave the house late at night to walk to the woods so she could be alone with God.

I will always remember my mother returning good for evil when my father was so cruel. I will always think back on how she would sing praises to God through her tears, and how no matter how difficult it was to put food on the table, she would thank God for the fact that her name was written in the Lamb's Book of Life.

I'm sure she had no idea that in so doing, she was setting up a conduit through which blessings would flow to her children, her children's children, and so on. All she was trying to do was survive, but her godly attitude was passed on to all seven of her children and all fourteen of her grandchildren.

Through her testimony, we see that one woman's obedience, good attitude, and faithfulness to God impacted dozens of people that we know of. Only through generations of time will the full consequences of her godly behavior be known. We can't know right now, but perhaps there's another Moses or Abraham in her bloodline.

What blessings is your behavior passing on to your children?

CHAPTER 3

MERCY IS NEEDED FOR THOSE WHO STRUGGLE WITH INIQUITIES

THE CAMP ON whether or not iniquities actually exist is divided. Some believe that all that is necessary for salvation is what was done at Calvary. They believe that once you are born again, no such thing as iniquity exists in your life. Others believe they exist, but that they themselves do not personally have any. There are also those who believe that they have them, but since God is a merciful God they aren't worried about their situation, claiming, "God knows my heart."

A lot of people are impatient with those who teach about family iniquities because they believe that people should be held responsible for what they do. They say that blaming our problems on a propensity to sin that they received from their parents or grandparents is just avoiding personal responsibility. This is understandable because the Me generation of the '60s, '70s, and '80s certainly blamed a lot of their woes on the way their parents raised them. To deny that iniquities exist is sheer ignorance and may indicate a certain amount of religious bigotry or self-righteousness.

One of the reasons that people don't believe that iniquity is any of their concern may be that sexual sins and addictions, especially for women, are particularly stigmatized by both Christians and non-Christians alike. Many times, those who are unsympathetic to people with iniquities have lived a righteous life themselves and have not suffered the degradation of an addiction or moral failure. It is easy, then, for them to not understand the shame and humility that people with family iniquities have suffered. The people who misunderstand exactly what an iniquity is don't understand how incredibly courageous one must be in order to overcome these iniquities. Overcoming sin that is both rooted in iniquity and that has become second nature is probably the most difficult thing a person with an active iniquity will ever do.

I know a man who battled with cocaine addiction off and on for years, and, in those times when he was not using cocaine, he was very self-righteous and condescending to those still in the throes of their addiction. His thinking was, "If I can do it, they should be able to do it too." You would think that because he struggled with the same issue, he would approach it from a place of mercy, but he didn't. As far as I know, he was never able to stay clean for very long, and is still an addict to this day.

Have mercy on those who are "ignorant and out of the way" (Heb. 5:2). Iniquities are the most "comfortable" sin that a person has because the tempter has successfully hooked so many members of their ancestry before. As a result, it truly becomes nearly second nature for them to sin in this manner. Please be patient with them, but at the same time make them responsible for their actions. One of my sisters struggled for a long time with drug and alcohol addiction, and it became evident that she could not help herself. We knew from her physical symptoms that unless we intervened, she would die. The entire family had weekly conference calls regarding her problems, and we all fasted and prayed for her for two months before deciding on a confrontation. Because we sought God and fasted on her behalf, we were able to approach her in a way that humbled her, and she was able to accept our help when we found her a treatment center.

A Word About Shame

For all the years that I was under the bondage of alcoholism, there was such a shame in me that I could hardly look at myself in the mirror. Part of this probably came, no doubt, from the humiliation I suffered as a child. Because my father brought such disgrace to the family, carrying a load of shame became ordinary for us. We were often humiliated in front of the neighbors when our father was arrested for public intoxication or for his violent and lewd behavior both inside and outside of our home. Several times the police came in their paddy wagon and roughed him up in front of our gawking neighbors before they loaded him into their vehicle, much to our embarrassment.

His idea of interior decorating was to tape the centerfolds from *Playboy* magazines around the top of the wall in the kitchen. This was to humiliate my mother. It brought much shame to us girls, especially.

I remember how embarrassed we all were when our pastor would visit. Once any of our friends visited our house—which wasn't very often—they never returned.

At church, we bore the stigma of being the poor kids because we often had to wear hand-me-downs previously worn to church by fellow parishioners' kids. There were many members of our extended family who ostracized us because of our father's behavior. From this, we learned that we were "less than" our friends and family.

Translate that into an adult ego, and it is easy to see why following the iniquity patterns of my father was an easy choice. Please understand me. I don't blame my father for my alcoholism. I opened those bottles, and I kept my addiction hidden so that I wouldn't have to face it. But having an example of alcoholism as a way to solve problems made drinking an easy choice when my marriage proved to be a great source of pain.

People with a shame base find hiding their sin a necessary choice, and it comes very easy to them. The incredible fear of being found out is what keeps them locked in their cycle of shame and addiction: the more they feel ashamed, the deeper they go into their addiction; the more they are addicted, the deeper the shame, and on and on and on it goes.

Former First Lady Betty Ford was confronted by her loving family when it was clear that her drinking had gotten out of hand. People with a shame base would only be driven further into their addiction because of the tremendous fear of the public humility of confrontation. I know that would have been the case with me.

I mentioned earlier about the stigma attached to moral failures, especially among women, and that is certainly one of the reasons why women are more likely to hide their sins. Women are also more likely to be socialized with a shame base. The statistics on sexual abuse of female children bear out the fact that many girls obtain a shame base early in their lives. This will have a lot to do with how she picks a future husband.

Men aren't exempt from this either. In fact, a man with a shame base will often choose to marry a woman who will dominate him in the same manner that he was dominated when he received his shame base.

That is why when you deal with people in your family who have iniquities, it is profoundly important to show a great deal of mercy. Please try to remember that their addiction or sin pattern is only a sign of a deeper issue, and shame is often the core problem. Therefore, please let the fruit of kindness guide you.

Being tolerant up to a certain point is also acceptable. Always remember that as a family member, you have certain rights and responsibilities to lead that person to a place of repentance so that he or she can receive the help that they need, but the most important thing is to be merciful.

Iniquity Is Not an Excuse to Sin

Iniquities are also not an excuse to sin. I can't tell you how many times I've heard Christians say, "I can't help it. God made me this way." No, sin made you that way. (See Psalm 51:5). Saying you are a certain way because God made you that way means you are unwilling to acknowledge that you need to change. You are responsible for your own behavior. Quite frankly, this excuse is a cop-out.

Some iniquities are more visible than others. Some, like marital unfaithfulness or drug addiction, are fairly easy to see. Others, like laziness, class envy, and unforgiveness, are much more difficult to detect. But make no mistake; they are just as dangerous to the born-again Christian as the ones that are visible!

Having an iniquity is no excuse for sin, especially after you learn how it can be eradicated. Even though we are responsible for dealing with the iniquities that we inherit—that is, we have an obligation to find out which ones are in our family and break their hold—we are *not* responsible for the sins of our forefathers. Let me say that again: We *are* responsible for allowing the iniquities of our fathers to pass from us to our children, but we *are not* responsible for the sins of our forefathers. Nor are our children responsible for our sins; they are only responsible for breaking the iniquities that we might have unwittingly passed on to them.

> In those days they shall say no more, The fathers have eaten a sour grape, and the children's teeth are set on edge. But every one shall die for his own iniquity: every man that eateth the sour grape, his teeth shall be set on edge.
>
> —JEREMIAH 31:29–30

Do you see what this says? In days past, our forefathers enjoyed sin and passed the inclination to sin on to us in the same way. But once we realize what sin has done to us through our forefathers, we can take the steps necessary to remove those iniquities from our lives. In fact, the Bible clearly says that if we have iniquities that we are aware of and yet leave unresolved, He will not hear our prayers: "If I regard iniquity in my heart, the Lord will not hear me" (Ps. 66:18).

Deuteronomy chapter eleven speaks to the parents of children born after the escape from Egypt. Because the new generation did not see the slavery from which they were rescued, this chapter admonishes those parents to follow all of the statues of the Lord in order to be an example. Deuteronomy 11:17 tells what will happen if they fail to instruct their children in this way:

> Then the LORD'S wrath be kindled against you, and he shut up the heaven, that there be no rain, and that the land yield not her fruit; and lest ye perish quickly from off the good land which the LORD giveth you.
>
> —DEUTERONOMY 11:17

But how then do we get rid of those iniquities that are plaguing us or our children? How do we break the power of iniquities over us and the generations to come?

There Is Something Powerful About Your Words!

When the children of Israel were delivered from Egypt, they were told that after they got to the Promised Land they were to proclaim their blessings as well as their curses (Deut. 11:29). We are to do that in order to break the grip of iniquity on our lives. First, we praise God for the blessings that we have received. Then we are to confess the iniquities that we have in our family line, even if we have not succumbed to them!

"Death and life are in the power of the tongue: and they that love it shall eat the fruit thereof" (Prov. 18:21).

But what does that mean? It means that you can choose to keep your present circumstances and your weakness in areas of sin, or you can choose to declare that the iniquities that have been visited upon you by your forefathers' disobedience to godly principals will be forever eradicated from your blood line!

Which would you prefer? I know that I would rather hand blessings and peace down to my children and grandchildren, along with all the other benefits that come with obeying God and His covenants. We love to give our children good gifts, and I hope you agree that giving them the ability to walk in freedom is one of the best gifts you can give them.

Declare today and purpose in your heart that your words will be life-giving declarations of repentance and purpose so you and your children can walk in the abundant life that God has planned for you to enjoy (John 10:10).

CHAPTER 4

THE MOST COMMON INIQUITIES

I TAKE THIS TIME now to introduce to you the most common iniquities. Some iniquities, like laziness, can lead to other iniquities, such as learned helplessness and poverty. Most iniquities prevent believers from living the life that Christ meant for them.

As you read through these pages, ask God to show you those that may require your attention and prayer. You might also want to jot them down for use later on in the book as you pray the Prayer to Discover.

Works of the Flesh

The following iniquities are named in Galatians 5:19–21 as "works of the flesh."

Adultery

Most people think that adultery is when two people, one or both of whom are married, have sexual intercourse with someone other than their spouse. But adultery is much more than that. Adultery is any intimate behavior, whether physical, emotional, or spiritual, that occurs outside of the covenant of marriage.

A few years ago, one of our public figures claimed that oral sex with a co-worker in his office was not "sex." He couldn't have been further from the truth. The covenant of marriage is a promise between two people to keep themselves only for each other. The definition of a covenant actually means that each party to the covenant promises before God to cover and protect the other party from everybody else.[1] They have a relationship that is so close that there is only room in it for them and God. Anybody else who gets more attention, devotion, or time is a threat to that marriage. Allowing friendships, luncheons, car rides, closed door meetings, and similar encounters with members of the opposite sex is a potential recipe for disaster and should be avoided at all costs.

Sex or fantasies about sex with someone other than your spouse, emotional abandonment of your spouse, and unholy emotional ties to someone other than your spouse need to be treated as adulterous in nature. In fact, emotional abandonment of a spouse is probably more difficult to repair than a short-term liaison that is for physical gratification alone, although both are toxic and destructive to a relationship.

Often when a marriage lacks vitality or intimacy, one or both partners may seek sympathy from a member of the opposite sex. The pain of their marriage is so extreme that they feel they must have some relief by unloading on a friend. This is very dangerous because many times it leads to emotional intimacy, which in itself is precariously adulterous and can end in a physical relationship as well.

Fornication

Most people believe that the concept of fornication is now acceptable, but this is only because we have lost our sensitivity to sin. However, sex before marriage is not a merely physical act with physical consequences like the risk of pregnancy and STDs. Rather, it is a grievous activity that means that one does not value something that God says should be valued.

Why does God's word call Esau a fornicator in Hebrews 12:16? It never says Esau had sex before marriage, but he was called a "fornicator" because he did not value his birthright above a bowl of soup. Those who have sex before marriage do not value this intimate activity in the way God meant for it to be valued.

Why would God make that rule? Why would He withhold such an enjoyable activity from unmarried people? The reason that the sexual union of two people in marriage is so precious to Him is that it is a spiritual likeness to His relationship with the church. Many times in His Word God speaks about Israel "playing the harlot". (See Jeremiah 3:6, 8 and Hosea 4:15.) She should have been faithful to the one true God, but with every new king or leader, it seemed the people chose a new god to idolize.

Fornication that is expressed as intimacy with someone outside the bonds of holy matrimony is a sin that separates one from God and is idolatrous in nature.

Uncleanness

The way to become clean is to have the blood of Jesus applied to our lives through repentance, baptism, and walking in newness of life. Through the renewing of the mind, we receive not only the ability to walk free from sin but to re-gain the sensitivity to sin that we lost due to our sinful nature as sons and daughters of the flesh. Uncleanness is walking in a state of sin that one is unaware of before salvation, but can also be found in someone who is saved if they continue to live in sin.

Lewdness

Lewdness goes hand in hand with uncleanness, except lewdness primarily involves improper sexual behavior. Those who have no conscience about improper displays of sexuality have also been desensitized to sin. They tend toward less and less restraint, as further desensitization occurs. That is why people who are drawn into the world of pornography find it so difficult to break the cycle of addiction once they are hooked. Once desensitization begins and the conscience is repeatedly ignored over time, more graphic and immoral images are needed in order to satisfy the spirit of lewdness.

Idolatry

Idolatry is another one of the sins that besets humanity. Many people don't even know what idolatry really is. They suppose that it is bowing down to or lighting candles for benign stone or wood figures at an altar. This is one definition of idolatry, but one can be guilty of this sin by simply putting people, relationships, things, or activities before God. Your spouse, children, hobbies, your physical appearance, home, image, job, and goals can all become objects of worship that exalts itself above the true and living God. (See Exodus 20:3.)

Sorcery

The sin of sorcery has been around for thousands of years and has recently become quite respectable. In the city in which I live, there's a sign at every other bus stop espousing the virtues of one of any number of psychic readers around the corner. Truly, as warned about in God's word, going to a psychic is wrong (2 Chron. 33:6), but most people don't know that merely controlling others by manipulating them or their circumstances is the same as the sin of witchcraft. Many Christians would never go to or send their children to a psychic or witch, but they have no trouble at all controlling people through money, emotional blackmail, or other forms of manipulation.

Parents must especially guard against manipulating their children. If they do this, then this verse bears attention: "Train up a child in the way he should go: and when he is old, he will not depart from it" (Prov. 22:6). Failure to heed this verse is a scary thought, because then the sin of sorcery will become the guidelines for their children's lives, and they will perpetuate it in their children as well.

Hatred

Hatred is unprovoked and intense hostility toward something or someone. John 3:15 says that if anybody hates, he is the same as a murderer. Perhaps God likens hatred to murder because hatred is often the precursor to murder. Hating people prevents us from ministering to them and showing them the love of Christ. God's Word tells us that the only thing we are to hate is sin, evil, and unrighteousness. (See Psalm 97:10 and Proverbs 8:13.)

Contentions

When someone is contentious, there is just no pleasing him or her. Time after time the book of Proverbs talks about the downsides to spending time with a contentious woman. (See Proverbs 21:19, 26:21, and 27:15.) Contentions are bullied assertions of one's own rights or opinions. In fact, Proverbs says that almost anything–even the tortuous, unending dripping of water (Prov. 19:13)—is better to be around than someone who is contentious. There is just no pleasing these individuals, and, once you try to, it becomes a slippery slope that only leads to hopelessness and emotional captivity. They are worse than pessimists, in that they carry more than just a negative attitude. It is negativity that leads to "unrighteousness, indignation, and wrath" (Rom. 2:8).

Jealousy

Bitter feelings, suspicion, or unhappiness because of another's possessions, relationships, or status is something that no particular age group seems to have a grip on. The Word of God states that in the last days, "The lust of the flesh, the lust of the eyes, and the pride of life," three components of jealousy, would be manifested in those who loved the world (1 John 2:16).

Jealousy has ruined marriages, separated friends, and instigated wars. A little bit of jealousy keeps one loyal and in pursuit of one's mate (2 Cor. 11:2), but the kind that causes strife, bitterness, or separates friends should never be present in the life of a believer.

Wrath

Wrath is different than mere anger because it has the added component of revenge. Anger simply means that the body has physically and emotionally reacted to an event or conversation. Regular exhibits of strong anger, usually expressing the desire for revenge, have been shown to produce illness and even death in those who practice it regularly.

Selfish ambitions

Trying to succeed without regard to the cost to others is called selfish ambition. Ideally, this is trait that should be worked out of us by the time we've reached high school age. Unfortunately, many people never get a handle on the fact that the earth does not revolve around them.

Many times selfish ambitions extend to marriage. One or both people in a relationship may find that, while they managed to succeed in obtaining the object of their selfish pursuits, it came at the expense their most valuable gift: the love of their spouse and/or children.

Dissensions

Dissension is a half-brother to contention, and is rooted in rebellion. It can be cloaked in many things, such as manipulation or deceit, and a person struggling with this iniquity has a tendency to disagree with most everyone.

Rebellion is as the sin of witchcraft and separates us from God (1 Sam. 15:23). The purpose of dissension is to create conflict, often to avoid the true subject of disagreement or to throw off blame.

Heresies

There is so much to say about heresies that it is impossible to list all the things that are heretical in nature. Basically speaking, anyone who embraces any teaching that is contrary to and condemned by God's Word is guilty of heresy.

During the Crusades, heretics were burned at the stake, stretched on the rack, beheaded, and tortured in unspeakable ways.[2] In other eras, including now, they have been tarred and feathered, drowned, publicly whipped, and hung. In some countries, Christianity is considered the highest form of heretical thinking and the punishment is decapitation and desecration of the body after death. Today, though, in the United States, diversity and "sensitivity" training is becoming mandatory in many corporations. I believe this practice is a covert attempt to legitimize sinful lifestyles that contradict the pure morality of the Bible. Sadly, not even a nod is given to those Christians in other countries who suffer horribly for the truth of the Gospel of Christ.

In order to avoid creating a volume on this subject alone, suffice it to say that anything that exalts itself against the knowledge of God and the finished work of Christ, is heresy. Those who want to rightly divide the Word of Truth and not be guilty of heresy should read and diligently follow 2 Corinthians 10:5:

> Casting down imaginations, and every high thing that exalts itself against the knowledge of God, and bringing into captivity every thought to the obedience of Christ.

Envy

Envy means to resent somebody else's success or good fortune due in large part to feelings of inferiority. When someone resents their own circumstances or feels guilty because they feel badly about someone else's better situation, the desire to possess what the other person has fuels an emotion that manifests as envy.

These sentiments can lead to the separation of friends, broken covenants, and even murder. Envy killed Jesus (Matt. 27:18), sent Joseph into slavery in Egypt (Acts 7:9), and caused Paul and Barnabas to be persecuted and run out of Antioch (Acts 13:45).

Murder

By definition, murder is the crime of deliberately killing another person.[3] However, the Word of God says that to hate anybody without cause is as the sin of murder. (See 1 John 3:15.) This same verse also states that anybody who hates his brother is committing murder in his heart against him and has no eternal life in him. So it could be understood that a person who hates his brother is a murderer, and by merely hating him, he is not a candidate for eternal life.

Drunkenness

This is the state of being intoxicated, and is more than mere social drinking. Of all the verses in God's Word that mentions drunkenness, the list of other sins in association with it are envy, murders, reveling, overindulgence, sorrow, desolation, rioting, and wantonness. Galatians 5:21 states that if anybody practices these things, they will not inherit the kingdom of God.

Revelries

People who enjoy wild, noisy, drunken parties are guilty of revelry. They go beyond mere drunkenness to the point that they totally live for the opportunity to abandon all sensibilities. This iniquity produces many things, including promiscuity, violence, unfaithfulness, and a change in the moral fiber of the individual. It means more than partying; it is lawlessness produced by a gradual numbing of core values and the eroding of moral fiber through the sins committed during the time they are under the influence of mind-altering substances.

Other Examples

The following iniquities are those that I have observed in our culture and are traits that I believe hinder a Christian from living an overcoming life.

Depression

Many people suffer from depression, and many times it is a result of self-hatred. Self-hatred can begin from several factors, either as a result of others who have projected their anger or dissatisfaction onto the person or of anger that is turned inward on oneself. When people behave differently than their internal moral compass dictates, internal dissonance may develop, beginning a cycle of self-loathing that is difficult to break. A person can become perpetually pessimistic, and the internal pain may become so difficult to handle that self-medicating with addictive substances like drugs and alcohol becomes an attractive solution. Depression may be grouped with fear as one of the most common iniquities, and it thwarts the potential of the person who is in its grip.

Grasshopper complex

When Joshua and Caleb returned from the Promised Land with the ten other spies, they proclaimed that the land was fair and was ready for the picking (Num. 13:27, 30, AMP). The other spies, however, declared, "We were in our own sight as grasshoppers, and so we were in their sight" (Num. 13:33). They discouraged the others from wanting to enter into the land that was theirs. This is a perfect example of the grasshopper complex and how the chronic feelings of being invisible or powerless hinder many people who suffer from this condition.

Having the grasshopper complex has nothing to do with truth or fact. Joshua and Caleb were not stronger, smarter, or more able than the other ten spies. They simply believed that they were able to take the Promised Land with God's help. Believing you are able to do something is the first step in actually doing it. Conversely, believing you can't do something will often become a self-fulfilling prophecy. Henry Ford said, "Whether you believe you can do a thing or not, you are right."[4] This is what makes the grasshopper complex so sad—capable people believe a lie about themselves that prohibits them from even trying. Many will go to their graves with their undeveloped potential, and having the grasshopper complex is one of the reasons why.

Fear

"And the sound of a shaken leaf shall chase them; and they shall flee, as fleeing from a sword; and they shall fall when none pursueth" (Lev. 26:36). Fear is probably the most common iniquity, and it is the single most powerful iniquity that can shape our lives. There is a healthy fear that healthy parents teach us—to look both ways when crossing the street or not to talk to strangers. But sometimes even good parents can unwittingly give us a fear base by not properly protecting us from the world around us. If in adulthood one is unable to properly handle the normal challenges of life, fear can become a crippling emotion that prevents an individual from developing into the person God intended them to be. God's Word says that He is not pleased with those who shrink bank in fear (Heb. 10:38–39, AMP).

Being held back by real or imagined, conscious or subconscious, fears and anxieties is debilitating and leads to a life of misery and frustration. However, the most devastating thing that can happen is that any of these factors can lead to acting out other iniquities, usually through self-medicating the misery with addictive substances such as drugs or alcohol. It is important to understand that the only fear that we should have is the fear of God. (See Deuteronomy 6:1–2.)

Laziness

Laziness is one of those things that often goes unnoticed, but is a huge waste of time, talent, and potential. People who are unwilling to work or to make an effort to work are leaving themselves open to a life that has a beginning and an end, but nothing in the middle. To be unmotivated in life is to totally waste all the resources God has placed in you, and those at your disposal.

The story in Matthew 25:14–30 talks about the master and the talents. When the master returned, the slothful (lazy) servant handed him back only what he had been given, while the other servants gave the master back more than he had left in their care. Because the servant had been lazy and had not produced anything from his talent, he was cast into outer darkness, forever separated from God.

Laziness can produce a cycle of poverty that is difficult to break, even with all the governmental resources available. If not broken, generations of depression and subsistence-level existence are the result. This makes it even more difficult to break, since all a person can see as far back as he looks in his family history is laziness, poverty, and a life of living on the edge of survival.

Suicide

Not all suicide results in physical death. Many people receive such a repository of negativism and spiritual bankruptcy that they have no restraint against living a life completely void of God's presence. Therefore, suicide includes all self-destructive behaviors or tendencies that end in spiritual, emotional, or physical death. This includes attitudes, heresies, atheism, New Age, addictions, as well as all methods of physical self-murder.

"And ye will not come to me, that ye might have life" (John 5:40). Jesus tells the simple reason why people are lost. In all their pursuing, they don't pursue Him, and in this simple ignoring of the provision, they choose death. This is spiritual suicide. When faced with life's many challenges, turning to Christ is the answer. Any other answer leads away from (eternal) life and brings spiritual death. Evangelist Fred Brown explains it this way:

> Believe it or not, or illogical as it may seem to logical minds, the only reason souls are lost is that they reject life. In the full knowledge of the consequences, under circumstances conducive to accepting Christ, millions today are premeditatedly, deliberately, with callused hearts, turning from Christ as the giver of life and committing spiritual suicide.[5]

Addiction

When people think of addictions, they think of things like drugs and alcohol. Very few realize that addictions can come in the form of devotion to a person, a substance, or any activity. This kind of devotion can also bring pleasure that is addictive, producing physical or psychological dependence that is difficult to break. Furthermore, all addictions are idolatry, because the initial pleasure that is produced takes the place of the comfort that God Himself wants to give.

Poverty

Poverty comes in many forms, some of which are financial, emotional, and spiritual. Someone who is financially poor is not always without money, a person who is spiritually poor is not always godless, and an emotionally poor person is not always single or lacking in other relationships.

Financial poverty is not just being unable to afford the basic necessities of life. It can, if you are not careful, become a state of mind. True financial poverty is the state of never having enough to take care of basic needs and the learned helplessness that accompanies this condition.

Spiritual poverty is the state of not having the *ability* to understand principals that lead to devotion to a higher power. This is often the result of physical, emotional, or sexual abuse. These things deny a person of the reality of who they are as a creation of God. Therefore communicating with Him and accepting Him as a loving Savior is difficult for them to understand.

Someone who has emotional poverty is also likely to have been a victim of some form of abuse. Their negative past experience either makes intimate relationships abhorrent to them, or they feel there is no need to love or be loved at all.

The "less-than" mentality

People with the "less-than" mentality never seem to feel good enough to progress past a certain point in life. They never feel they deserve help, praise, or promotion. Consequently, they miss all the opportunities that come their way to better themselves in their careers or relationships.

People around them seem to have some hidden secret that they themselves can't seem to tap into, so depression, bitterness, and a negative attitude set in. This outlook creates a cycle as their negativity will validate their lack of progress, further discouraging them from pursuing success and prosperity. The "less-than" mentality is one of the most difficult iniquities to overcome, but when one gets a handle on it and walks away from it, he or she will see the greatest results in lifestyle change.

The "me-me" mentality

The "me-me" mentality is the tendency to believe that the world owes you something. A person who suffers from this selfish proclivity never feels responsible for his or her own individual actions, especially ones of failure. They are very resourceful in fabricating scenarios that prove that they are not, in fact, at fault for things that go wrong. Instead, they believe that others are out to get them. This iniquity happens when someone gets stuck emotionally, usually from trauma during childhood, and still exhibits all the selfishness of that emotional age, no matter how many years have elapsed since that trauma. These people are extremely hard to deal with because their center of reference is inward and selfish, while a healthy individual's is outward and unselfish.

Jezebel women

Jezebels are women who hate and browbeat men, publicly or sometimes only privately. Jezebel women get what they want by going around or above the heads of the male authorities in their lives. (See the story of Jezebel in 1 Kings 18, 19, and 21.)

Recently a lot has been preached about the Jezebel woman because it has affected so many congregations. Whole cities have been affected by the Jezebel spirit inhabiting and ripping apart a good body of believers.

The true sin of the Jezebel spirit is that it cuts off the inheritance from the father to the children.

Anything that prevents the natural or spiritual inheritance of the fathers (parents) from being properly handed down to their children involves the Jezebel spirit. We see this in 1 Kings 21, where we read that Jezebel's husband, King Ahab, desired Naboth's vineyard. Naboth refused to trade it or sell it to the king because it had been in his family for years and was set to be his sons' inheritance. Ahab seemed to respect that Naboth wouldn't sell what was meant to be his children's inheritance. Jezebel, on the other hand, had Naboth killed so his property could be confiscated. This is the sin of Jezebel—cutting off the inheritance from father to son (or daughter).

Anything that prevents spiritual advancement in your bloodline, especially through marriage, could be the Jezebel spirit. The thing to remember is that there can't be a Jezebel without an Ahab. It was never recorded that King Ahab punished his wife for this despotism. Because of this, he set up his own children to be robbed of their spiritual destinies.

Weak men

Many times men who end up being weak and ineffectual are men who were raised by and end up marrying Jezebel women. These important female figures in their lives belittle and demean them to the point of emotional evisceration. Whether their wife took their authority from them, or whether they surrendered it voluntarily, they are prevented from being the true priest of their home.

If the father in the home is weak and ineffectual, sons will be set up to walk in the footsteps of their father, and daughters will learn to rule their own husbands. This iniquity could be easily eliminated if only men and women would welcome God's sovereign rule in their lives, walking into marriage with a true covenant heart and allowing the headship of the family to be the man and the headship of the man to be Christ. In the case where a woman is the single head of household, the Word says: "For your Maker is your husband, the LORD of hosts is His name" (Isa. 54:5, NKJV). This being true, she would defer her authority to Christ. In any case, Christ should be the head of the house and His principles of authority should be honored so that the children will have the heavenly Father as an example.

Chronic complaining

Proverbs 18:21 states: "Death and life are in the power of the tongue and they that love it shall eat the fruit thereof." Through personal observation, I have found that people who are chronic complainers tend never to get to the place that their talents should be able to take them. With an attitude of "nobody ever does anything right," these people are difficult to be around, and fairly soon after meeting new people they are running them off with their negative attitude and behavior. Nothing suits them, including people who try to befriend them. They are suspicious in nature, and because they see the glass as half-empty, they filter all their relationship dealings through negativism and emotional penury.

Shame

Many people suffer from what is called a "shame base." Shame is different from guilt. Guilt is a natural reaction to one's own wrongdoing. Toxic shame is a learned reaction to what is done to an innocent person.[6] Childhood emotional, sexual, and physical abuse are the major causes of shame, in that the adult perpetrating the abuse manages to blame the victim for the abuse.

This is also often true when a woman is the victim of rape: She is blamed for tempting her attacker because of how she was dressed, where she was, or what she was doing. Shame is always caused by another and has nothing to do with guilt, although having shame can cause a person to feel guilty as well. One must understand that, while guilt is a healthy reaction to sin, shame is never healthy. It should never be felt by anyone who is the victim of any type of abuse. Shame is simply unjustified feelings of dishonor, unworthiness, and embarrassment that come upon a victim at the hands of others.

Sickness

Many people would be doubtful if you said that sickness is an iniquity that may be easily identified by observing what families suffer from. Is it any coincidence that at the first visit to a new doctor, he asks for a family history of disease? One might say that it is merely a physical thing, not a spiritual matter, that is being passed down from one generation to another. But if you or your family members are suffering from or dying of the same things that your ancestors died from, then there might be a sin component that needs to be considered.

Original man was without sickness. It was only after the fall that sickness pervaded mankind. How did it get there? Jesus came across a man who was blind since birth, and his disciples asked, "Who sinned, he or his parents?" (John 9:2, author's paraphrase). Even though in this case the cause of the blindness was for the glory of God to be demonstrated, we can see that the disciples thought that sin was a normal thing to question when someone was sick. In Acts 10:38 we are told that Jesus went about "healing all those who were oppressed of the devil." There is also a spirit of infirmity that manifests itself in the language of a person who constantly claims they are either sick, just catching, or just getting over an illness. It is as though they enjoy ill health, using their on-again, off-again symptoms as an excuse never to succeed. In my experience, this phenomenon is an offshoot of the iniquity of fear and learned helplessness.

In his book *A More Excellent Way*, Pastor Henry Wright asserts that "some diseases are genetically inherited, but some are 'spiritually rooted.'"[7] I agree. Pastor Wright uses many years of ministry research to biblically prove the sin-sickness connection. He has identified scores of illnesses related to spiritual disobedience, including cancer, Parkinson's disease, addictions, migraines, and diabetes. The iniquities of fear, unforgiveness, complaining, hatred, and bitterness are causes for disease, says Pastor Wright. People often remain unhealed of physical disease until the underlying iniquity is rooted out of their lives.

This is not to say that all illness is strictly due to an iniquity, but even attitudes and lifestyle choices like smoking, drinking, poor eating habits, and avoiding regular checkups can be passed through families. Repeating these poor decisions of your parents may increase your chances of suffering from the same diseases that they had by exacerbating symptoms.

Bitterness

Bitterness is a serious iniquity, for it allows the actions of others to keep someone depressed and angry. Bitterness is the core reason behind why many people never get past a certain stage of success in their life. They have very good reasons why they don't get what they want. Their vocabulary usually includes superlatives like *never*, *always*, and other words that seem to prove why something else has prevented them from succeeding. Bitterness comes from a me-centered ego that is masked by cynicism and protected by anger.

Gossiping

In order to root gossiping out of our lives, one must recognize that gossiping involves talking about others in any way other than to speak highly of or praise them. Telling someone a tidbit of information about someone "so they can pray for them" is merely a façade for gossip. It should never be done unless speaking to a pastor or counselor in a professional setting, or in the unlikely event that someone may hurt themselves or others.

Backbiting

Backbiting is a malicious conversation that leaves no doubt as to someone's feelings about another. Even more dangerous than verbal backbiting is the body language or "knowing look" that damages the intended target. Why are these gestures and implied accusations so damaging? They are never easy to defend or confront! The perpetrator of a knowing look can simply deny their actions and claim innocence, while the victim or witness to this behavior becomes confused and starts to doubt themselves. To say hateful things about somebody behind their back is vicious and produces rumors and accusations that cannot be easily stopped once started. (See James 3:5–6.)

Anger

Anger is a spiteful spirit of anxious annoyance without justifiable cause, and people who have a lot of anger usually have it for many reasons other than what their words reveal. Anger can be a symptom of a broken emotional outlook or an unhealthy view of God, borne out of perceived mistreatment by Him. It is a stronghold that usually defends another, deeper issue, such as fear or shame. It destroys friendships, marriages, and creates other human misery, such as wars and murders.

Self-defeating behavior

The fear of success can be one of the biggest fears to overcome. Self-defeating behavior is manifested in different ways, including constantly setting oneself up for failure. Fearing success is one way in which people never press through to the life Christ meant for them to have. For them, the space between deciding to succeed and actually seeing the fruits of that success is sometimes a scary, lonely place.

Many people decide they want to succeed, and they launch themselves into the place where success can be apprehended. Then they begin to shrink back in fear by subconsciously doing something that ensures failure. In their hearts, they recognize that with success comes new responsibility and acclaim. Although they may want these things, they fear it on some subconscious level, so they push any potential success away.

Self-defeating words

Self-defeating words predict failure—they become self-fulfilling prophecies. The primary motivation for this is fear. The manifestation of self-defeating words is the same as self-defeating behavior. These people never do anything to bring about success. They just talk it to death. Have you ever heard words to this effect? These are examples of how someone expresses a desire to succeed and then defeats themselves before they even start:

ॐ "I've always wanted to start my own business, but most businesses fail within the first two years."

ॐ "One day I'd like to learn to water ski, but I've never been very athletic."

ॐ "I know enough about my hobby to write a book about it, but since I don't have a college degree, nobody would publish it, let alone read it."

The Word says that "death and life are in the power of the tongue: and they that love it shall eat the fruit thereof..." (Prov. 18:21). This means that the words you say are seeds into your future–what you plant, you will eventually harvest. (See Job 4:8.) People who say they will never succeed or that they can't do this thing or accomplish that thing will harvest that action from the words they plant. Again, whether you believe (or say) you can, or believe (or say) you can't, you are planting seed for those very outcomes.

Coveting

Coveting may best be explained as simply desiring something that belongs to someone else, especially if you have not earned it or can never rightfully have it. In this day and age, everyone wants everything they see—the latest and greatest phone, game station, or tech toy. We are consumed with consuming, and things that used to be luxuries have been elevated by our greed to the point of perceived necessity. 1 John 2:16 states it like this: "For all that is in the world, the lust of the flesh, and the lust of the eyes, and the *pride of life*, is not of the Father, but is of the world" (emphasis added). If we could do as the author of the book of Hebrews recommends, to be "content with such things as ye have" (Heb. 13:5), we would not be guilty of coveting the things of this world. After all, only the things that are not seen will last. (See 2 Corinthians 4:18.)

Child abuse

Our society focuses on the physical and sexual aspects of child abuse, but there are many forms other than that, including emotional and spiritual violation. David Henke defines spiritual abuse as, " . . . the misuse of a position of power, leadership, or influence to further the selfish interests of someone other than the individual who needs help."[8] Spiritual abuse in its most general sense is not necessarily abuse by religious authority—it is *any type* of abuse by *any type* of authority that wounds the human spirit.

My siblings and I suffered from severe neglect of our physical needs, in that we didn't have enough food to eat or proper clothing to wear. However, the most damaging abuse was emotional and spiritual, as it left us unprepared for proper decision-making as adults. The emotional abuse taught us not to challenge the world around us, accepting only the mediocre choices we were presented and living with a "less-than" mentality. It was the spiritual abuse and wounding in my childhood by my father that made me doubt myself and my ability to believe that I was someone who should be valued. That is why I married the first person who asked me. I felt I was fortunate to have been chosen at all. Many of my siblings and I married people who could not protect and cover us spiritually and emotionally. Some of us perpetuated the doormat syndrome of our mother and became victims of physical abuse as well.

Child abuse is also the primary gateway for instilling shame into a person. It is the main reason people never achieve their dreams—if they even dare have them—and why they end up purposeless, defeated, bitter, and angry. Abuse and its consequences produce emotional, spiritual, and even physical sickness and can result in an early death that could have been avoided, had the proper needs been met in childhood.

Dishonesty

Dishonesty has many names: cutting corners, hedging the truth, telling white lies. The tendency to be deceitful for personal gain in any area is the iniquity of dishonesty. Some people, due to shame and lack in their childhood, have an unspoken and unacknowledged belief that life owes them some-thing. Therefore, anything gotten by subterfuge or craftiness is all right by them.

Dishonesty is another type of seed that bears fruit. Just like words of death and defeat produce failure in one's future, any gain that comes at the expense of honesty actually creates lack. This principle is explained in Proverbs 11:24: "He who scatters, yet increases more; And there is one who withholds more than is right, But it leads to poverty." By "letting go, and letting God" bring to you what is rightfully yours, you will have much more than if you use dishonesty to create a cushion of security for yourself.

We should always remember that the principles of the kingdom of God are opposite those of the world, which instruct us to save all we can, invest, and pay ourselves first. God's way is a way of giving away in order to get, sowing into others to reap for yourself, and dying to yourself to be able to live with Him forevermore.

Learned helplessness

Emotional and spiritual abuse teaches an indi-vidual that their circumstances will never change, no matter what he or she does, and sets children up so they are never able to help themselves as adults. I remember once seeing a photo in a psychology textbook that really gave me pause. It was a photo of a young girl who had been severely abused and neglected. She was a pretty little girl, but the look in her eyes was so sad that I could hardly view it. I thought it was just sadness, but seeing this photo in an article on learned helplessness taught me that there was more.

What was so startling about it was that I had seen that look on my youngest sister Gail's face—a look of being resigned to fate, hopeless and unable to move out of emotional paralysis to enjoy the more noble pursuits of life. Like shame, learned helplessness creates a cycle of hopelessness that prevents individuals from reaching their true potential.

False humility

Humility means having a proper view of yourself and of your station in life. Unfortunately, it must be learned, while pride—which causes a person to exalt himself—is a feeling that can develop without any effort on our part, almost naturally. We can never truly get humility right. When we try, our psyche keeps correcting us back to pride because that is our nature.

False humility can result from this struggle, among other sources. It is a phenomenon wherein one attempts to mask feelings of worthlessness and insecurity with self-deprecating humor, without actually being humble. False humility may also arise from being taught that we should not take credit for any of our accomplishments, but must concede that God did it or that it's what anybody else would've done. By not allowing ourselves to be acknowledged for personal accomplishments, we perpetuate the self-esteem issues that prompt us to display false humility in the first place. Thus, pride remains an unchallenged giant in our life when we attempt to mask it with false humility, so as not to *appear* full of pride.

Family secrets

Knowing about sin patterns within the home but never discussing them with anyone outside of the family is the primary way that iniquities go on for generations. Even when abuse or addictions are obvious to neighbors, friends, and other relatives, a sense of shame can prompt families to ignore these patterns, keeping the secrets hidden. Many times, when people grow up and talk to their extended family about what they endured, the aunts and uncles admit that they knew something was happening but were afraid to interfere.

Through the influence of TV reality and talk shows that encourage participants to tell all, people are revealing more to each other of what goes on behind closed doors. Still, sins that are of a sexual nature are still generally hidden, though they are perhaps even more common than they were in the constrained decades of the past.

God's Word tells us in Ephesians about all the works of the flesh and that these things should be exposed by the light.

> But fornication, and all uncleanness, or covetousness, let it not be once named among you, as becometh saints; Neither filthiness, nor foolish talking, nor jesting, which are not convenient: but rather giving of thanks. For this ye know, that no whoremonger, nor unclean person, nor covetous man, who is an idolater, hath any inheritance in the kingdom of Christ and of God. Let no man deceive you with vain words: for because of these things cometh the wrath of God upon the children of disobedience. Be not ye therefore partakers

> with them.... But all things that are reproved
> are made manifest by the light: for whatso-
> ever doth make manifest is light.
> —EPHESIANS 5:3–7, 13

Once revealed, God can begin to heal those who will allow these things to be removed from their lives.

Covenant breakers

There was a time not so long ago that businessmen could shake hands and seal a deal, sometimes for millions of dollars. In those days, a man's word was his bond. By now, we all know that we live in a world where promises have little or no meaning. Some politicians may say one thing to get elected, then vote the way they want once installed in office. The court system has years of backlogged cases, and current statistics indicate that around fifty percent of all marriages end in divorce.[9] According to the *Barna Research Group*, Christian marriages have slightly *higher* divorce rates compared to members of other faith traditions, atheists, and agnostics![10] In our society, if one of the parties to a contract doesn't believe he or she should be limited by what they formerly agreed upon, they take action to dissolve the agreement, rather than honoring their word.

God is the God of authority, and He is saddened by our ignorance about why it is so important to be faithful to an agreement we enter into, whether it be a legal contract, like a lease agreement or business partnership, or a verbal contract such as promising our children to take them to the park on Saturday.

Marriage is the most important covenant of all. God instituted marriage for (at least) two purposes:

to produce a godly seed (Mal. 2:15) and to give us a type and shadow of His relationship with us. It is in this intimate relationship that we fulfill God's longing from the beginning: to have someone to fellowship with and to love. When we satisfy the yearning that He has for us, we automatically satisfy and validate our own reason to exist.

The children of Israel were constantly reneging on their covenant with God. Even though he bought them back over and over again, they never truly recognized their responsibilities as covenant partners with Him. The Old Testament speaks about their "whoredoms," or unfaithfulness in seeking after other gods (Jer. 13:27), showing us how grieved God was (and is) by anyone who has entered into covenant with Him and fails to honor that agreement.

The same is true with some Christians today. After our initial experience at the altar, we often don't allow God to affect a heart change in us. Because of that, we don't live any differently than the ungodly people around us! We have entered into a marriage covenant with God, but we are still carrying on an affair with our old partner! In a recent message by prophetic intercessor Dutch Sheets, he explains this covenant breaking as "two-timing," and cites that it is one of the biggest reasons the financial blessings of God have not fallen on the Church.[11]

This list may seem overwhelming to you at first, and you may feel that you have too many to address all at once. Don't worry, that is fine with God! He is such a gracious God that He is willing to allow you to deal with them as He brings them to your attention. I have found that working on self is like peeling an onion; you only do it one layer at a time. God is faithful to show you what you need to work on first, so let Him show you the ones that need the most immediate attention! Later on in the book you will discover where to begin on this journey.

CHAPTER 5

WHAT ARE THE RESULTS OF UNRESOLVED FAMILY INIQUITIES?

INIQUITIES ARE RESPONSIBLE for many of the woes that plague our families and relationships, and they obstruct the life goals of millions. Many of these kinds of iniquities lead to lifestyles of devastation from generation to generation, such as:

- $ a cycle of poverty that seems impossible to break; never getting ahead;

- $ child abusers raising children who abuse their children;

- $ generations of broken families/single parenting;

- $ children out of wedlock;

- $ losing one's children to "the system" (i.e., foster care, termination of parental rights, lost custody);

- mental illnesses;

- physical illnesses, such as cancer, heart disease, diabetes, and other lifestyle-related diseases;

- resigning oneself to a lifetime of being mistreated;

- believing fate has been unkind, yet feeling incapable of striving for a more satisfying life;

- eating disorders, such as anorexia and bulimia;

- a fear of new people, places, and events (agoraphobia);

- personality disorders;

- multi-generational criminal behavior;

- children who are rebellious and/or incorrigible;

- individuals who are talented and gifted, but never realize their potential;

- unable to leave unhappy, dangerous, or stressful relationships;

- failure to thrive in any area of life; disconsolate; living, yet waiting to die;

      the inability to dream because hopes have been dashed too often.

King David

King David said: "Behold, I was shapen in iniquity; and in sin did my mother conceive me" (Ps. 51:5). In other words, part of what his mother was is what he became, not only in the natural, like the color of his hair, skin, and eyes, but the spiritual—the propensity for certain types of sin.

David *coveted* another man's wife, Bathsheba, and he committed *adultery* with her while her husband Uriah was off at war. When David found out that Bathsheba was pregnant with his child, he tried to trick Uriah into believing the child was his own. When that plan didn't work, he arranged for Uriah to be put in the front lines of battle so he would be killed. David's sin led him to be guilty of *murder*, as well as covetousness and adultery (2 Sam. 11:2–24). David's *arrogance* showed when Nathan, a prophet, came to visit. In response to the prophet Nathan's parable about the rich man who stole the poor man's lamb, David became angry with the rich man in the parable and said that he should die for his actions (2 Sam. 12:1–6). However, David was so blind to his own sin that he didn't realize that the prophet was talking about David's sin with Bathsheba.

All you have to do is read the story of two of David's sons, Amnon and Absalom, to see the repetition of David's unrepented sins, which he passed on as iniquities. Amnon repeated his father's covetousness and sexual sin when he desired and then raped his half-sister (2 Sam. 13:1–14). Absalom continued his father's sin by having Amnon murdered for violating his sister (2 Sam. 13:28). He also practiced sexual sin with his father's concubines (2 Sam 16:21–22) and showed his arrogance when he rose up against his father and led an unsuccessful rebellion against him, thinking that he should be ruler over David (2 Sam 16:16–18:9)

David's story and his passing on of iniquities to his sons is an example of what *not* to do. You must note, though, that Amnon and Absalom had to act out this unchecked iniquity in order for it to have this effect upon them. They had a choice. They could have repented and denounced their father's iniquities before it took a toll on them, but they completed the iniquity by acting out their father's sin. James 1 describes the cycle into which they fell:

> Let no man say when he is tempted, I am tempted of God: for God cannot be tempted with evil, neither tempteth he any man: But every man is tempted, when he is drawn away of his own lust, and enticed. Then when lust hath conceived, it bringeth forth sin: and sin, when it is finished, bringeth forth death.
> —JAMES 1:13–16

Another thing I noticed in this story was that David apparently never disciplined Amnon after Amnon raped his sister. He banished Absalom after he killed Amnon, but that was not the same as punishing him for the murder, which in those days would have been death. David's lax attitude toward the sin in his house could have been one of the contributing factors in the ungodly end of his other son, Solomon, the wisest, yet the most foolish man who ever lived.

Discover, Confess, Repent, Announce, Declare

How are iniquities broken? First, earnestly ask God to reveal to you those unbroken iniquities that have been in your bloodline. He will be faithful to show you. Ask Him to bring to your remembrance situations and stories that you remember about your parents, grandparents, aunts, and uncles. You may have to spend time pondering some of them to understand what God is showing you, but He will show you.

Next, look at your brothers, sisters, cousins, and your children (if you have any) and see if there is a pattern of behavior and attitudes, either in lifestyle or life status. These are clues as to which iniquities might be in existence in your family.

Once you have knowledge of one or more iniquities, the first thing to do is to ask God to forgive you and your ancestors for being unwilling or unable (by ignorance) to break these iniquities. Let me pause here for just a moment: Remember, you are not repenting for your ancestor's sins. This is impossible to do. They must do that or have done that for themselves. What you are doing is the same thing that the priests and the Israelites did when they repented: the priests asked for forgiveness for the sins and iniquities of the nation of Israel; the heads of families did the same for the people in their households. There was something about repenting for the nation that brought the priest to a place of audience with God that he could not have gotten to without that repentance. The same applies to you as you lift your family up to the Lord.

The first thing you must do is ask God to forgive your ancestors for not breaking the bonds of iniquity on you and your family. Next, announce that these revealed iniquities, as well as those you don't yet know, have no more power over you. Declare that your children and their children (and so on) will not feel the effects of their forefathers' sin. This is a very important part of your prayer, and should be declared each time new iniquities are revealed to you.

Once you have *discovered* your family iniquities through fervent prayer, *confess* that your family has been guilty of these iniquities and ask God to *forgive* you and your ancestors for not breaking them up until now. *Announce* that these iniquities no longer have any power over you and *declare* them broken over you and your children. Next, you need to ask God to reveal to you the blessings that have been stopped because of the iniquities present in your bloodline.

I was amazed at what God revealed to me when I did this. Some of the iniquities in my bloodline were: depression, suicide, addiction, the grasshopper complex, the "less-than" mentality, sickness, shame, self-defeating behavior and words, child abuse, poverty, and dishonesty.

Once I discovered, confessed, repented, announced, and then declared that these iniquities no longer belonged to me or my bloodline forever, I asked God to reveal what my family had missed because of these continued propensities for sin. I was amazed, because for each iniquity present in a bloodline, there is a blessing that has been held back. The following verse paints a picture of the spiritual concept of iniquities.

> For all the wells which his father's servants
> had digged in the days of Abraham his father,
> the Philistines had stopped them, and filled
> them with earth.
> —GENESIS 26:15

In this verse, the earth that fills in the wells is representative of the sinful nature of man, and it indicates how iniquities stop up the reservoir of our blessings. Let's see what happened when Isaac unstopped those wells:

> And Isaac digged again the wells of water,
> which they had digged in the days of Abraham
> his father; for the Philistines had stopped
> them after the death of Abraham: and he called
> their names after the names by which his
> father had called them. And Isaac's servants
> digged in the valley, and found a well of fresh
> water there.
> —GENESIS 26:18–19

Isaac discovered new streams of water, or blessings, when he undid what the enemy had done to him and his family. We do the very same thing when we remove the iniquities from our bloodline.

Once I discovered the iniquities and began to break their power over me and my family, I began to see some of my family starting to walk in these blessings. It was then that I was able to grasp the power of what I had done by breaking our iniquities.

Some of the blessing that God began to release were: success in business and the power to create wealth, public ministry, the ability to inspire others, respect, credibility, confidence, healthy boundaries and relationships, and proper God-centered self-esteem. Previously dormant gifts began to surface, such as: prophetic understanding, literary creativity, dream interpretation, words of knowledge, and discernment.

The enemy does not want you to have God's provision of an abundant life: "The thief does not come except to steal, and to kill, and to destroy" (John 10:10, NKJV). My iniquities did almost kill me. Don't let your iniquities stop up the wells of your family's happiness and success. Read the following prayers, and get them into your spirit. As you pray to the one true God, Jesus Christ, He will be faithful to forgive and remove your iniquities. He will also release the blessings that heretofore you have not been able to realize. "I have come that they may have life, and that they may have it more abundantly" (John 10:10, NKJV).

CHAPTER 6

TIME TO PRAY

NOW YOU ARE ready to begin. The three prayers that follow will help you discover which iniquities are keeping you from being all God meant you to be. Pray the Prayer to Discover, and once God begins to reveal them to you, list them on a sheet of paper.

After you've discovered those issues that you need to deal with, go to the second prayer, the Prayer to Confess and Repent. There is power in this prayer! When you humbly admit to God that you have been wrong—even innocently wrong—you obtain an audience with Him that you could not have had before. Take your time as you let God know that you realize you have broken His heart through disobedience. There is something sweet to Him when you come to Him like a child in true repentance.

Next pray the Prayer to Announce and Declare. This is where you release yourself, your children, and your children's children from the effects of generational iniquities. This is powerful, and yes, it works even if your children are grown and out of the house. They must accept responsibility for their actions and be willing to make a change, but you will have done your part by breaking the cycle in your generation.

After you have prayed these prayers, you can expect to begin receiving some of the blessings that your family has forfeited because of the iniquities handed down to you. If you will pray them regularly, it will be easy for God to show you any additional issues that He desires to reveal to you. Soon you will have all of these committed to your heart so that you may truly pray them with your spirit, rather than just speak the words intellectually.

You are on your way! God bless you as you press in to His grace and mercy.

The Prayer to Discover

> *Dear heavenly Father, I acknowledge that I was born in sin, and I thank You for the blood that cleanses me from all of my sins. I ask You right now, by the authority given to me by the blood and name of Jesus, to reveal to me those iniquities that have been in my family for generations that have kept me and my family from breaking through into the place of destiny that You have planned and desired for me.*
>
> *Let Your will be done in my life, here on earth as You have already planned in heaven. In Jesus' name, amen.*

Once God begins to reveal your family iniquities to you, list them on a sheet of paper and periodically pray the next series of prayers.

The Prayer to Confess and Repent

Dear Heavenly Father, I confess the iniquities of _____ in my family, and ask that You forgive me and my ancestors for turning our backs on You during the time we were enjoying our sin. I realize that it has kept us from a closer walk with You. I ask you to forgive our iniquities and remember our sin no more, according to Jeremiah 31:34. In Jesus' name, amen.

The Prayer to Announce and Declare

Dear Heavenly Father, because of Your many promises and tender mercies, I announce by the authority of Jesus' name that all iniquities that were ever a part of my family are now broken over me, my children, and my children's children.

I declare that I am free from the iniquities of my forefathers, and I also declare that these iniquities are forever broken from me, my children, and my children's children. In Jesus' name, amen.

CONCLUSION

FRIEND, IF YOU prayed these prayers, then those things that have always held you back are now broken over you. Don't take them back by having negative words or thoughts. All you need to do now is to keep declaring that you are free from the power that iniquity has had over your life, the lives of your children, and those who have gone before you. It is a powerful thing to speak those words of freedom.

After you do, you are authorized to help remove the chains from other people's bloodlines. Jesus has put all things under His feet by His death on the cross. (See Hebrews 2:8.) Since you are a part of His body, then all things are under your feet as well.

Once you understand how powerful your words are over your family's iniquities, you will never look at these failings and sin patterns the same way again. Jesus gives us the authority to overcome all evil by the blood of Jesus, and by the things that we say. (See Revelation 12:11.)

Remember that once these iniquities are broken you can start to speak to those blessings that have been kept from you and your family. Just like my mother's willingness to serve God through the worst kind of abuse brought her a godly seed—that is, her obedience brought about a spiritual transformation in her posterity which bore good fruit—you too can release the blessings that have been reserved for you by determining to start right now with your generation to serve Him no matter what.

I often marvel at the power that is within words: By merely speaking, God brought the worlds into existence. The word of God, when heard by individuals and mixed with faith, can do the most difficult thing in the world: change a person's mind. Let your words be mixed with faith as you announce and declare into the second heaven[1] that you are free, and God will release those blessings that He so desires to give you.

Let each man say "I am free!" For he whom the Son sets free, is free indeed. (John 8:36.)

EPILOGUE

IN THE YEARS after my father left, one thing that my mother did had a large impact on the family: she never spoke harshly about the husband that had treated us all so cruelly. Instead, she had us all pray for him, that God would somehow reach him in a way that she could not do while they were still married. We were never allowed to say one bad word about him, however true our accusation might have been.

After one stint in the state hospital (back then, alcoholism was considered a mental illness) and two stretches in the county jail, he fled to another state to avoid paying any of the child support he owed for his seven children. (He never paid any of it, choosing instead to quit his UAW job as a skilled tradesman to avoid paying it, even when he had only three years to go before full retirement.)

Coincidentally—or maybe not—he moved to Clinton, Oklahoma, which was within a few hours of where I then lived. Over time, I was able to re-establish a relationship with him. Because of my mother's refusal to allow anyone to speak evil about him, my siblings and I had long ago forgiven him for all the wrongs he had done to both us and our mother.

Working as a menial laborer, he drifted from job to job, living first in his car and then a series of flophouse apartments with his new wife. He put caps on bottles at the local Coca-Cola factory, worked as a garbage man and dog catcher, and then finally landed a job as a custodian at the local Assembly of God church. It was there that he renewed the faith of his childhood and found God in a new and lasting way. He was finally able to buy a small house, and I was able to visit him every few months.

Over the years, we developed a close relationship and we would talk for hours, sometimes at his house, sometimes holding a fishing pole over the side of his boat. Man, was he proud of that little boat with its stubborn outboard motor! I can still remember how proud he was of me when he saw that I wasn't too squeamish to put worms on my hook!

But the good times could not last. Two years after he gave his life to the Lord, he found that his lungs were filled with cancer, and a year after that he went home to be with the Lord.

During the weekend he died he kept telling Jesus he was ready to come home. I knew Dad had changed, but I wanted something tangible to tell the rest of the family when I finally had to convey the news that he had died. Except for my oldest brother, Howard, I was the only one who really knew Dad because they all still lived in Ohio, and I lived close enough to visit him often. I knew that there were still skeptics in our family about the condition of his soul, so I asked God to show me that His mercy had indeed been extended to my father.

So when Dad asked me to pray for him, I did so gladly. The day was dark, with thunder clouds that only Oklahoma skies can produce. It had rained all day and not a hint of the sun had shown itself, even though it was past three o'clock in the afternoon. The storm was raging so badly that the curtains were pulled closed in case the wind blew out the glass.

I closed my eyes in prayer and asked God to receive my Dad into His arms, and to take away any fear he might have. I could sense him letting go by the lessening of the tension in his grip, and I knew that God was comforting Him as only He can.

As I stood at his bedside in the peace that enveloped the room after the prayer, I opened my eyes to see that a shaft of light from the sun had somehow made it through a small chink in the curtains that were closed tight, landing in the middle of his chest, right at his heart. I knew that I had gotten confirmation that God had extended His hand of mercy to my Dad, and that I could tell the rest of my family that he had made it into the Lamb's Book of Life. Dad passed away the next morning, and I know that he was merely transported into a new dimension, the one that this life is only preparing us for.

When I speak to people who have had to deal with impossible situations where there is no money, no peace, and no hope, I tell them about my Dad and how he made it into heaven through the chaste conversation of my mother. I also tell them that by uncovering and confessing their own iniquities they will produce heavenly consequences that they cannot imagine while they are going through it.

I've learned that nothing just happens. God has already written our book (Ps. 40:7), and it is up to us to find out what it is that He has always intended for us to do with our lives. In that process, we find the substance of who we are and our purpose—even if that means pain and hardship. During our quest to find out who He intended us to be, He pours sweet healing into us, which we in turn can pour out to others. That, indeed, is something worth passing on to the next generation!

Appendix: Iniquities Quick Reference Chart

Addiction	Devotion to a person, substance, or activity that brings pleasure and produces physical or psychological dependence that is difficult to break
Adultery	Sex or fantasies about sex with someone other than your spouse; emotional abandonment or betrayal of your spouse (telling someone else about the private goings-on in your marriage), unholy emotional ties to someone other than your spouse
Anger	A spiteful spirit of anxious annoyance without justifiable cause
Backbiting	To say hateful things about somebody behind their back
Bitterness	Lets the actions of others keep them depressed and angry and serves as an excuse to never succeed
Child Abuse	Physical, sexual, emotional, or spiritual violation of a child

Chronic Complaining	Believes that nobody ever does anything right; nothing suits them
Contentions	Bullied assertions of one's own rights or opinions
Covenant Breaking	Doesn't keep promises, ignores or does not honor contracts, agreements, or legal matters including marriage and business responsibilities
Coveting	Desiring something that is someone else's, especially without earning it or that can never be yours (a career for which you are unsuited or unwilling to work for; someone else's spouse, etc.)
Depression	Self-hatred, anger turned inward; perpetually pessimistic
Dishonesty	Cutting corners, hedging the truth, telling white lies; the tendency to be deceitful for personal gain
Dissensions	A tendency to disagree with most everyone; rebellion
Drunkenness	The state of being intoxicated; more than mere social drinking
Envy	Resenting somebody else's success or good fortune, such as class envy
False Humility	Masking feelings of worthlessness with self-deprecating humor without actually being humble; related to pride

Family Secrets	Knowing about sin patterns within the home, but never discussing them with anybody outside of the family; this is the primary way that iniquities go on for generations
Fear	Being held back by real or imagined, conscious or subconscious, anxieties; this is the most common iniquity of all and can lead to acting out other iniquities (especially self-medicating behaviors)
Fornication	Sex before marriage; not valuing any thing that should be valued (i.e., Esau was a fornicator in that he did not value his birthright over a bowl of soup).
Gossiping	Talking about others in any way other than to speak highly of or praise them
Grasshopper Complex	Chronic feelings of being invisible or powerless
Hatred	Unprovoked and intense hostility toward something or someone
Heresies	Embracing teachings contrary to, and condemned by, God's Word or orthodox doctrine
Idolatry	Putting people, relationships, things, or any activity before God
Jealousy	Feeling bitter, suspicious, or unhappy because of another's possessions, relationships, or status

Jezebel Women	Women who hate and often openly browbeat men. Jezebel women get what they want by going around or above the heads of male authority figures in their lives.
Laziness	Unwilling to work or to make an effort to work; unmotivated
Learned Helplessness	Learning that no matter what one does, their circumstances will never change; resigned to fate
Lewdness	No conscience about improper displays of sexual behavior
Murder	Crime of purposely killing someone; to hate without cause
Poverty	The state of never having enough to take care of basic needs, and the learned helplessness that accompanies this condition
Revelries	The acts of enjoying wild, noisy, drunken parties
Self-Defeating Behavior	Constantly setting oneself up for failure; fearing success
Self-Defeating Words	Words predicting failure that become self-fulfilling prophecies
Selfish Ambitions	Trying to succeed without regard to the cost to others
Shame	Feelings of dishonor, unworthiness, and embarrassment

Sickness	Suffering from or dying of the same things that your ancestors died from; always either sick, just catching, or just getting over an illness
Sorcery	Controlling others by manipulating them or their circumstances; witchcraft
Suicide	Self-destructive behaviors or tendencies that end in spiritual, emotional, or physical death
The "Less-Than" Mentality	Never feeling good enough to progress past a certain point in life; feels they don't deserve help, praise, or promotion
The "Me-Me" Mentality	Always feeling the world owes them something; never feeling responsible for their own actions, especially failure
Uncleanness	Comfortable with and unbothered by sin
Wrath	Regular exhibits of strong anger, usually expressing the desire for revenge

About the Author

ALI STABLEY WAS born in Toledo, Ohio, the middle of seven children, to Donald and Marian George. She is a graduate of Mt. Zion Ministry Training School and is a licensed minister with Evangel Association of Churches and Ministries (EACM) in Roseville, Michigan. Ali is married to Garth, inventor of Terra-Kleen®. They have two children, Chase, an Eagle Scout and Air Force Cadet who lives in Michigan, and Lisa, an account services representative, who lives in Texas with their grandchild, Ian.

Ali is an Acts 2:4, Spirit-filled Christian, who believes that God has called her specifically to minister to hurting women and those whose relationships have been injured because of family iniquities that have never been dealt with and removed. She believes that to be without hope is devastating, so she speaks and writes to encourage those in the most hopeless situations that God can and will intervene in their circumstances if they will only cry out to Him, believing that He can help them, and seek the counsel of others who have gone before them. (See Hebrews 11:6.) Ali encourages people to proclaim that the power of iniquities is broken, so that they may be released from the bondage of sin patterns, no matter how devastating or how long they have been present in a family's bloodline.

The Spirit of the Lord GOD is upon me;
because the LORD hath anointed me
to preach good tidings to the meek;
He hath sent me to bind up the
    brokenhearted,
to proclaim liberty to the captives,
and the opening of the prison
to them that are bound;
To proclaim the acceptable year of the LORD,
and the day of vengeance of our God;
to comfort all that mourn;
To appoint unto them that mourn in Zion,
to give unto them beauty for ashes,
the oil of joy for mourning,
the garment of praise for the spirit of
    heaviness;
That they might be called trees of
    righteousness,
the planting of the LORD,
that he might be glorified.
And they shall build the old wastes,
they shall raise up the former desolations,
and they shall repair the waste cities,
the desolations of many generations.

                —ISAIAH 61:1–4

Notes

Chapter 2—What Is an Iniquity?

1. *Encarta Dictionary Online*, s.v. "curse," http://encarta
.msn.com/dictionary_1861602031/curse.html (accessed
October 29, 2005).

2. Ali Stabley, 1992.

3. Morton Kelsey, *Reaching for the Real*, (Pecos, NM:
Dove Publications), 1981.

4. Untitled sermon, May 6, 2003, Call From the Mountain Audio Productions, Clarkston, MI, 2003.

Chapter 4—The Most Common Iniquities

1. Bishop David Huskins, *The Power of a Covenant
Heart*, (Shippensburg, PA: Destiny Image Publishers,
Inc.), 2000.

2. John Foxe, *Foxe's Book of Martyrs*, (New York:
Fleming H. Revell Co., 1989).

3. *Encarta Dictionary Online*, s.v. "murder," http://
encarta.msn.com/dictionary_/murder.html (accessed
October 28, 2005).

4. *Quoteland.com*, s.v. "Henry Ford," http://www.quote-
land.com/author.asp?AUTHOR_ID=974 (accessed July
16, 2007).

5. Fred Brown, "Why So Many Commit Suicide," http://
www.swordofthelord.com/archives/WhyManySuicide
.htm (accessed July 8, 2007).

6. John E. Bradshaw, *Healing the Shame Base That Binds
You*, (Deerfield Beach, FL: Health Communications, Inc.),
1988.

7. Henry W. Wright, *A More Excellent Way: Be in Health, Spiritual Roots of Disease, Pathways to Wholeness*, (Thomaston, GA: Pleasant Valley Publications), 2003.

8. David Henke, "Spiritual Abuse," *The Watchman Expositor*, http://www.watchman.org/profile/abusepro.htm (accessed July 5, 2007).

9. *Religious Tolerance.org*, "US Divorce Rates for Various Faith Groups, Age Groups, & Geographic Areas," http://www.religioustolerance.org/chr_dira.htm (accessed July 16, 2007).

10. Ibid.

11. Dutch Sheets, "Contending with Baal," http://joshua1.wordpress.com/2007/06/12/contending-with-baal/ (accessed July 16, 2007).

Conclusion

1. Tony Capochia, *Bible Bulletin Board*. s.v. "Heaven." http://www.biblebb.com/files/HEAVEN.HTM (accessed October 29, 2005).

To Contact
the Author

§   For information about Ali's schedule or to engage Ali to speak at your next Women's Conference or Seminar, write to info@alistabley.com.

§   Send your testimony to testimonies @alistabley.com.

§   For more information visit www .alistabley.com.

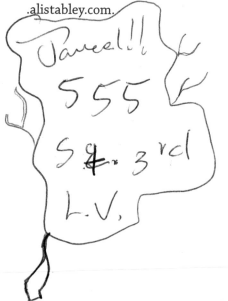